DIARY

OF A MINECRAFT STEVE AND HIS OCELOT

BOOKS KID

TABLE OF CONTENTS

Day 1 1

Day 2 3

Day 3 6

Day 4 8

Day 5 10

Day 6 14

Day 7 17

Day 8 19

Day 9 22

Day 10 24

Day 11 26

Day 12 30

Day 13 32

Day 14 36

Day 15 40

Day 16 43

Day 17 45

Day 18 47

Day 19 49

Day 20 52

Day 21 53

Day 22 55

Day 23 59

Day 24 60

Day 25 64

Day 26 66

Day 27 67

Day 28 69

Day 29 72

Day 30 74

Day 1

My name's Steve and I live in a place called Minecraftia. One of the best things about living here is that you can build all sorts of things.

I live in a shelter that I built all by myself. It's totally awesome! It has five bedrooms, an enormous kitchen and a bath as big as a lake.

OK, maybe the bath isn't quite as big as a lake, but it's still pretty big. More like a swimming pool than a bath. I could have the best pool parties.

The only problem is that I don't have any friends. You see, I built my shelter in an area that seems to get a lot of monsters. I don't know why, but zombies, witches, creepers, you name it. If it's mean and scary, then you'll find it somewhere close to my house.

I don't mind. I quite enjoy having battles with monsters. But other Minecraftians don't like having to fight their way through monsters to come and visit, so they don't bother.

It gets quite lonely after a while. Have you ever tried having a pool party with nobody there? It's no fun. I've lost count of the number of times I've sent invitations out, got the food all ready and sat there waiting for everyone to turn up, only to have the sun go down and I'm still alone with enough party food to last a month.

I suppose I could move and build a shelter somewhere else, but I like living here. It's a beautiful part of the world and there are so many resources to be found. There's a mine not far from where I live, so it's easy to get all the diamonds I want and then bring them back to my treasure room.

One day I'm going to have enough diamonds to create a diamond museum. There will be diamond statues and diamond books and everything you can imagine made out of diamond, all kept in a building full of diamonds. That's the one good thing about living in a monster infested area – nobody knows just how many diamonds I have here so they don't try to steal them.

Still, it gets quite lonely being here by myself and the creepers are a real pain. It's really annoying when you have to rebuild half of your shelter because one of them decided to explode.

Day 2

It can get really boring mining diamonds after a while, so this morning I decided to take a break and do something exciting.

Fishing!

What do you mean, fishing isn't exciting? It is the way I do it. I lure creepers towards the water and get them to blow up to kill the fish. So far, I haven't been able to catch many fish this way, but it sure is a lot of fun.

I don't know why people are afraid of creepers. As long as you don't get too close to them, they aren't a problem. I guess that Minecraftians don't have the skill I do. I'm sure I'd get more visitors if there weren't as many creepers here, but then again, I wouldn't have so much fun fishing.

I did some normal fishing as well, just to make sure that I had enough food for dinner. I did really well and soon I had more fish than I could possibly eat.

I took them home and put them in my pantry before going back to the mines for more diamonds. Usually, I can go straight to the seams and dig them out, but today was different.

As I drew closer to where I'd stopped mining last time I was here, I heard a strange, skittering sound.

CHITTER CHATTER CHITTER! CHITTER CHATTER CHITTER!

Uh-oh. Whatever was making that noise, it wasn't going to be good.

I pulled out my trusty enchanted sword and crept towards the sound. Nothing was going to get between me and my diamonds.

I peered around the corner and my heart sank at what I saw.

Three spider jockeys.

Skeletons were bad enough, but put them on top of a spider and it's even worse. This was going to take more than just a sword.

I checked my pockets and was relieved when I found a couple of splash potions of slowness. That should give me the edge.

"YAAAAAAAAAARRRRRRRRRRRRRRRRRR!!"   I leaped out from my hiding place and raced towards the spider jockeys.

SPLASH! CRASH! I threw the potions of slowness and got lucky, hitting two spider jockeys with one potion and getting the other one square in the face. I immediately followed it up with some cuts and thrusts, getting in some direct hits on the spiders and skeletons.

This battle was going to be over almost as soon as it had begun.

This was where having a shelter in the heart of monster territory really helped. I had plenty of experience in fighting monsters and even if spider jockeys were more difficult than many of the monsters I'd faced, they were no match for me.

Soon they lay around me, while I had barely a scratch on me. At last I could get my diamonds.

HISSSSS! BANG!

The blast of an explosion hit me and I fell into a dark, dark sleep.

Day 3

At last I awoke, my health almost gone. Luckily, I also had a potion of healing with me. I drank it and felt better straight away. Those creepers! I hadn't even heard it coming. I was so focused on fighting the spider jockeys, it hadn't occurred to me that there might be anything else to worry about.

I gave up on looking for more diamonds and slunk back to my shelter to rest. Maybe I should move after all. I was getting tired of having to fight monsters all the time.

Enough is enough. I decided to head out and scout for a new location for my shelter. First, I needed to make sure that no one was going to steal the diamonds I'd spent so long collecting. Just because there were lots of monsters in the area didn't mean that some nasty thief wouldn't try to get to my treasure.

I set up a number of land mines around my shelter, placing TNT around the building with hidden pressure plates so that it would be difficult to get round them to my diamonds. I threw in a few pit traps as well, just to keep people on their toes. My diamonds would be safe until I was ready to come back for them.

Once I was happy that I'd protected my shelter as best I could, I packed my bag with plenty of supplies so I was prepared for whatever I came across. Then I set off to find a better place to live. When I had my new shelter, I'd come back for my diamonds.

Day 4

I walked in a direction I'd never been in before and I was curious about what I might find there. My shelter was in a forest with mountains to the north and I'd spent most of my time exploring these, sometimes venturing over to the Extreme Hills to gather emeralds when I needed to trade with the local villagers.

This time, I was going south and I had no idea what I was going to discover.

After walking for a while, I began to regret not finding a horse. Walking was really boring. Still, after my fight with the spider jockeys the other day, boring was better than exciting. I would be very happy if I didn't have any excitement like that for a while.

At last, I decided to set up camp for the night. I was in no mood to fight any more monsters, so I built a simple shelter in a clearing in plenty of time for sunset. It was nowhere near as impressive as the large house I'd left behind, just a simple wooden structure with four walls and a door, but it would be enough to keep the zombies out until daylight.

I lit a fire just outside the door and took out some fish to cook. I had to admit that eating food cooked over a campfire tasted a lot better than it did in my big kitchen at home. I don't know why. It's not as though I added any extra flavor.

As I munched on my fish, I thought about what might happen tomorrow. Would I find the perfect place for my new home? Maybe I'd make some new friends. That would be awesome!

Day 5

For once, I slept all night without any monsters banging on my door, trying to get in. That made a pleasant change. Still, this place wasn't exactly right for my new permanent home. It was a bit damp and it didn't smell very nice.

I packed up my things and set off. As I walked, it became wetter and wetter and muddier and muddier, the trees hanging over blocking out the sun.

I was in a swamp!

I'd never been in a swamp before. This was a new adventure. If I moved my diamonds here, they'd definitely be safe. Nobody would want to wade through the swamp water to steal them. On the other hand, one of the reasons for moving was to try and make new friends. I couldn't imagine many Minecraftians would to trek all the way out here just for a cup of tea together.

"What have we here?" cackled a voice behind me.

I whirled round to see a witch standing in front of me.

"I don't get many visitors all the way out here," she said. "Which is a real shame. There's nothing like Minecraftian stew made with real Minecraftians!"

Minecraftian stew! I didn't like the sound of that.

"Much as I love the sound of that, I'm afraid I'm in a bit of a hurry, so if you'll excuse me, I'll just be on my way."

I started to edge my way round the witch, hoping that I could run away, but she pulled out a potion from her robe and threw it at me.

SPLASH!

It hit me straight in the face and I could feel my strength ebbing away. I pulled out my sword, but I could barely lift it. It was just too heavy.

"Oh yes. You'll do very well for my stew." The witch came forward and pinched me on the arm, testing to see how much meat there was on me.

"I'm. Not. Going. To. Be. In. Your. Stew."

I summoned what little strength I had and reached in my backpack for a potion. I didn't bother to check what type it was – I knew that I didn't have much time before the witch finished me off. I was just going to have to hope that whatever potion I'd found would be enough to help me defeat her.

Gritting my teeth, I threw it at her with all my might. The potion landed straight in her face, releasing its contents.

"Aaaaarrrgghhh!" she screamed. "It burns! It burns! I'm melting! I'm melting!"

Burning AND melting? That was one impressive potion! Obviously she had been weakened by a battle moments before I crossed her path and hadn't had enough time to regenerate because witches are much stronger than that.

She was no match for me and soon the witch was defeated. "No more Minecraftian stew for you!" I crowed.

The potion she'd thrown at me had been very powerful, so I decided to see if I could find her hut. Maybe she'd have enchanted weapons or other strong potions I could take with me.

It took a while of wandering around the swamp, but at last I found her hut, overlooking a smelly pond. I held my nose as I went in. I definitely wasn't going to build my new shelter in the swamp. My nose would fall off!

There was very little furniture in her hut, but I took a look in the chest in the middle of her room. Jackpot! A whole heap of potions, as well as a few ingredients and a very nice enchanted bow. Perfect for adventuring.

It was getting late and I decided to spend the night in her hut. It would be safer than sleeping out in the swamp.

I locked the door to her hut and then put the chest in front of it for extra security, but even knowing that nothing could get in, I struggled to get to sleep. There were too many strange noises outside. Maybe the witch wasn't the only one living round here. What if there was a whole coven of witches and they were gathering to get revenge on me for killing their sister?

The sooner I got out of the swamp, the better.

Day 6

I must have had about half an hour's sleep with all the tossing and turning I did. Worst night's sleep of my life.

As soon as the sun was up, I took down the barricade and left the hut. The sooner I was away from the swamp, the better.

I hurried off, continuing to head south. Hopefully the swamp wouldn't go on for too much longer.

As I walked, it became hotter and hotter, the swamp gradually drying up and eventually disappearing completely. There was no doubt that I was heading into a new biome, unlike anything I'd ever seen before. Even the sky seemed lighter.

The trees were bigger here, the trunks twice the size of anything I'd seen before. Some of the trees seemed so high, they almost touched the sky! I stopped at the foot at one and looked up, but I couldn't see the top.

If I decided to rebuild my shelter here, there was certainly plenty of wood I could use. Unlike the dirty greens of the swamp, everything was a beautiful green and I felt happier just being in the sunshine surrounded by stunning views.

The land was becoming quite hilly and as I made the way to the top of a hill, I got a good look at the landscape around me. I'd found a jungle!

I'd heard of jungles before, but I'd never been in one and I was very excited about what I might find. I'd heard that a fruit called a melon grew here. I'd always wanted to see what one tasted like picked straight from the ground. By the time I'd traded for one, they were quite old. I bet they taste amazing when they've just been plucked from the ground.

There were lots of the tall trees around, making it difficult to see too far into the distance, but through the trees I thought that I could see the glistening blue of some lakes. Where there were lakes, there were bound to be fish, which was good. I was running low on supplies and fish was my favorite food.

I headed down the hill, into the jungle. The floor was covered with leaves, making a squelching noise as I walked over them.

SCRUNCH! SCRUNCH! SCRUNCH!

It was really dumb of me, but I wasn't paying attention to where I was going. I was too excited about looking around me, taking in all the new and exotic plant life. I didn't notice the vine that had grown across the path until it was too late.

I tripped over it, stumbling forward and banging my head on a tree.

Everything went black.

Day 7

I was dreaming that I was being chased by zombies. They were all around me in the jungle, moaning and groaning as they slowly shambled after me. I reached for my trusty sword, but it wasn't in its scabbard and all I had to defend myself was a bit of rotten meat.

I waved it at the zombies, but all it seemed to do was make them angrier. They surrounded me, reaching out to grab me. I felt one of them lick my cheek, tasting to see how delicious I was.

"No! Don't eat me!"

My eyelids fluttered open and I realized that something really was licking my cheek!

"Aargh! Get off!" I waved my arms and the creature ran away. I just caught sight of the end of a tail disappearing around a tree.

Very strange. If whatever it was had wanted to eat me, it had plenty of chances while I'd been knocked out. Was it licking me to try and wake me up?

Whatever it was, it was gone now and I'd probably never see it again.

Day 8

I can't shake the feeling that something's watching me, but every time I look around to see who it is, there's no one there. Maybe I'm imagining it.

My supplies were running low so I decided to spend a nice relaxing day fishing. I could get used to the jungle life. There's something very soothing about listening to the exotic birds and the weather's certainly very nice. Lovely and hot.

I'd brought my fishing rod with me just in case I got the chance to do some fishing and I headed off to the nearest lake. There were plenty around, so I figured that if I didn't have much luck finding fish in this one, I'd move on to the next until I found a spot where the fish were biting.

Making myself comfortable, I threw out the line and settled back to wait for a fish to take the bait. And waited. And waited.

After a while, it became clear that this was not a good place to fish, so I packed up my things and moved on to the next lake.

This was more like it! The fish were practically jumping out of the water at me, begging me to pick them up and have them for dinner. I'd be enjoying a feast tonight!

Every time I caught a fish, I put it in my backpack, but after a while I noticed something odd. Although I was having a lot of luck in catching fish, they seemed to be disappearing from my bag. Were they somehow managing to get back into the water?

The next time I caught a fish, I decided to try something sneaky. I put it in my bag and pretended to start fishing again. I heard a rustling in the bushes, and when I thought the fish thief was close enough, I spun round.

"Caught you!"

I don't know who was more surprised, me or the ocelot that was rummaging around in my backpack. I thought it was another Minecraftian!

The ocelot turned tail and sped off into the undergrowth before I could do anything. Good thing too. It had eaten six of my biggest fish. I'd been looking forward to those.

I settled back to fishing, making sure that I kept my bag close by. But as I fished, I started thinking. I'd been really lonely all this time and even though I'd left my shelter to find somewhere new to live, I still hadn't found anyone I could be friends with, just more monsters.

I wondered whether the ocelot I'd just seen was the same creature that had woken me up after my fall. If it was, then it was clear that it didn't want to hurt me. I'd always wanted a pet. Perhaps I could tame it. It would be really cool if I had an ocelot by my side to help me fight monsters.

Day 9

Once I'd had the idea of taming the ocelot, I couldn't stop thinking about it. The ocelot seemed to like fish, so I spent the rest of the day fishing and when I cooked my dinner, I made plenty for the ocelot as well.

All I had to do was sit and wait patiently for it to arrive.

I went back to the lake where I'd last seen it. Settling down, I waited quietly for it to arrive. Sure enough, eventually I heard some rustling in the trees. I held my breath, not wanting to make the slightest of sounds that might scare the ocelot.

At last, the ocelot poked its head out of the bushes. Success!

I held out a piece of cooked fish, but the ocelot didn't seem interested. "Come on, you silly cat," I muttered. "You ate plenty of my fish yesterday. Look. It tastes really good." I took a big bite out of the fish and held it out to the ocelot, but it ran away!

What was the problem? I chewed on the rest of the fish as I thought and then it came to me. The fish the ocelot had stolen had been raw. Like an idiot, I'd cooked all the fish and now the ocelot didn't like it.

Oh well. I'd just have to spend another afternoon fishing. Good thing that was one of my favourite things to do!

Day 10

The next day I went back to the same spot where I'd seen the ocelot and sat down under the tree. Opening up my backpack, I took out five raw fish. I took a sniff of one. Ugh! It smelled disgusting! Still, if that's what the ocelot liked, it would soon find me if it just followed the smell.

I waved it around in the air, hoping the fishy aroma would waft its way to the ocelot. Once more, I heard more rustling in the bushes as the ocelot cautiously made its way towards me.

"That's it. Good ocelot," I whispered as it poked its nose through the bushes.

I held out the fish, putting it on the ground just in front of the ocelot. It took a while to work up the courage, but finally it reached out a paw and hooked the fish. I could hear it crunching away in the bushes, enjoying the meal.

I pulled out another fish, leaning forward to wave it at the bushes where the ocelot had been. Again, the ocelot poked its nose out, sniffing at the fish to make sure that it was food and not some trap. Carefully, I put it on the floor and the ocelot swiped it into the bushes.

I hoped this was going to work. Otherwise, the ocelot was getting fat on all my hard work and all I was getting was sore knees from leaning forward to offer it fish.

There was a little yip from the bushes, which I took as a sign that the ocelot wanted another fish. I got another one out. This time, instead of putting it on the floor, I decided to see if I could get it to take it from my hand. I leaned forward, trying to coax the ocelot out of the bushes, but it was too shy.

Gradually, I edged closer and closer, holding out the fish at arm's length.

Suddenly, with a snarl, the ocelot snatched it from my hand. I could hear it running off into the jungle, taking its prized fish with it.

Looks like ocelot training was over for today. Still, I felt as though I'd made a real connection.

Taming an ocelot was going to need a lot of fish, so I spent the rest of the day fishing to restock my supplies. Stretching out and relaxing under the tree while the fish took the bait was the perfect way to spend an afternoon.

I could definitely get used to jungle living. This was just like being on holiday!

Day 11

The ocelot came a lot earlier today. It was as though it knew that I was going to be there with fish. These creatures are a lot more intelligent than I thought.

This time, I kept hold of the first fish I offered. If the ocelot wanted free fish, it was going to have to come and get it.

I stayed perfectly still as a little ocelot nose came sniffing through the bush. The fish was just outside of its reach, so eventually, its nose was followed by its head. It snarled when it saw me, but I didn't react. I didn't even look it in the eyes as I remained like a statue, hoping that the ocelot would take the fish.

My arm was aching with the effort of holding up the fish, but finally the ocelot took it from me, disappearing back into the safety of the bush to eat it.

I shook my arm, trying to get some feeling back into my hand after spending so long holding up the fish. When I thought the ocelot had finished eating, I got out another fish and held it out for the ocelot.

26

This time, it came forward sooner, which I was grateful for. I didn't know how long I'd be able to stay there holding out fish without my arms falling off!

When it took the fish, it ate it right in front of me instead of going off to hide. We were definitely making progress.

Carefully, I took another fish out of my bag, moving slowly so that I didn't scare the ocelot. It looked up at me at the sound of my bag opening and I froze, hardly daring to breathe in case I frightened it.

A moment later, it went back to its meal and I eased another fish out, ready for when the ocelot wanted more.

"Meow!"

The ocelot looked at me, as if to say "where's my fish, then?"

Slowly, I reached forward with the fish, hardly daring to believe my luck. It looked like I was going to have a tame ocelot!

I braced myself for the ocelot to snatch it away as it had all the other fish. But this time, it took the fish gently, blinking slowly and nodding at me almost like it was thanking me.

As it ate the fish, something amazing happened. The ocelot turned into a cat! Its markings faded away, becoming black and white. I had a tuxedo tom cat!

When it had finished eating, the cat came over and rubbed itself against me, purring. I stroked its back as it walked around me and when I stopped stroking, it batted its head against my hand, demanding that I show it more attention.

I picked it up and held it in front of my face. "What are we going to call you then?" I asked it, not expecting a reply.

"Meow!" it said.

"Wow. You might not speak Minecraftian, but you certainly know what I'm saying, don't you?"

"Meow!" it nodded.

"All right then. Let's see if I can figure out your name. Tom?"

The cat growled.

"Sam?"

Growl.

"Jack?"

Growl.

A thought hit me.

"Tabitha?"

"Meow! Meow! Meow!"

She wasn't a tom cat at all. I had a girl cat!

"Tabitha it is."

Tabitha purred and settled on my lap to go to sleep. I stroked her, watching the sun go down across the lake. I couldn't remember the last time I'd felt so happy.

Day 12

Now that I had my new pet, I decided to explore a bit more of the jungle. I'd spent so long trying to tame Tabitha that I hadn't really had time to have a proper look around. I bet there's lots of treasure to be found. Maybe even more diamonds!

"Where shall we go, Tabitha?"

The cat trotted a little way down a path and then turned to look back at me. "That way, you say? All right. That way it is!"

As I walked, Tabitha amused herself by jumping on the little patches of light that were filtering through the trees. I don't know what she thought she'd do with them if she caught any, but she seemed to be having fun.

"Wait a minute, Tabitha. What's that?" I could see a strange plant through the trees and I left the path to see what it was. As I got closer, I couldn't believe my eyes. It was a melon! A real melon!

I pulled one of the melons off the plant and used my axe to chop it in half. "There you go, Tabitha." I offered half to the cat, but she didn't seem interested. "Oh well. All the more for me."

I took a bite. Oh. My. Goodness. I'd never tasted anything so juicy in my life. "Are you sure you don't want any of this, Tabitha? It tastes amazing."

Tabitha growled at me, so I took a piece of fresh fish from my bag and tossed it at her. She caught it before it even hit the ground, disappearing off to a corner of the clearing to eat.

The melon juice dripped from my chin as I took large bites. There really wasn't anything like eating fresh fruit straight from the vine. Whatever I'd traded for melon in the past it was too much. It had never tasted anything like this.

When I'd finally eaten as much as I could stomach, I picked a few more fruit to take with me. Not too many – they wouldn't keep very well. But I knew where to come to get more and while I was living in the jungle, I'd be eating like a king.

The idea of staying in the jungle was more appealing every day I was here.

Day 13

Tabitha woke me up bright and early the next day by licking me on the face. I must admit that there are nicer ways to start the day. This was one habit I was going to have to try and get her out of.

"All right, all right." I pushed her off and opened up my bag to give her some more fish, while I had some melon for breakfast. It still tasted good the day after I'd picked it. Maybe I'd find some other exotic fruits while I was out here.

"OK, Tabitha. What adventures are we going to have today?" Tabitha looked up at me, her head cocked to one side as she considered the best place to take me next.

Eventually, she turned around and led me out of the makeshift shelter I'd put up for the night and off deeper into the heart of the jungle. We walked for what seemed like hours deep into the heart of the jungle.

The trees grew closer here and despite the brighter light of the jungle sky, it was dark as the sun struggled to filter through the leaves. "Are you sure we should be going in this direction, Tabitha?" I asked. "I've got a bad feeling about this place."

Tabitha ignored my worries, striding off ahead until she reached the edge of a clearing.

"Meow!" She turned around to look at me, nodding her head in the direction of something up ahead.

When I caught up with her, I could see what she was excited about. In the middle of the clearing was a strange building. "What is this place?"

"Meow!" If Tabitha knew what it was, she couldn't tell me, since I didn't speak cat. Still, I appreciated her effort to try as I slowly walked closer to the construction.

It was obviously very old, the stones grey with vines growing over them. It looked like a temple to a strange, ancient god of some sort. Steps led up to an entrance, the door wide open with a dark, dark corridor leading off.

It looked like a door into death.

"I don't know about this, Tabitha," I said. "Come on. Let's go and explore over here instead."

I turned to leave the clearing, but Tabitha meowed at me and jumped up the first few stairs. She sat half way up the temple, licking her paws as if she didn't have a care in the world.

"Suit yourself." I turned my back on her and walked off, but as I left the temple in the background. I had second thoughts. I didn't want Tabitha to get into any trouble and if I left her alone, who knew what might happen?

Sighing, I turned around and went back to the temple.

"Meow!"

"All right, Tabitha. I've come back. You don't need to be like that. I'll come into the temple."

"Meow."

"But not today. It's getting late and there could be all sorts of monsters in there. Look at it. It looks like a monster's dream home. No, I'll make a shelter nearby and we'll come back here first thing in the morning."

"Meow."

"I don't care if you think I'm being a chicken." I could tell that Tabitha wanted us to spend the night in the temple, but there was no way I was going to do that. It was far too spooky!

It didn't take long to build a shelter and Tabitha curled up at my feet to sleep for the night. I wished that I could sleep so easily. I was beginning to wish that I was back in my old shelter. There might have been zombies and creepers, but they were my monsters and creepers. I knew where I was with them. I didn't like the thought that there were strange jungle creatures lurking around, just waiting for the chance to leap out and gobble me up.

Day 14

"OK, Tabitha. This is it." I clutched my sword tightly, looking up at the entrance to the temple. My heart beat faster as I crept up the stairs, trying to work up the courage to go inside. I had visions of large monsters with countless tentacles and teeth as big as my head just waiting to drag me to my doom.

"Meow."

"All right, all right. I'm going as fast as I can." That wasn't true. In fact, I was deliberately going slowly, trying to delay the moment when I would have to go into the temple.

At last, I stood at the entrance, looking inside. A few steps led down into a lobby. I listened carefully, but I couldn't hear anything that sounded like a big tentacle monster.

"Meow!" Tabitha jumped down the stairs and disappeared off into the darkness.

"Tabitha! Come back here!" I raced down the steps, my fear momentarily forgotten, not wanting to lose the cat in the depths of the temple.

I swear that cat was laughing at me. I found her sitting in the middle of the room, sitting up proudly, her head cocked to one side as she looked at me standing in front of her.

"OK, you were right. There aren't any monsters here. At least, not in this room. Even so, I want you to stay behind me from now on, all right? I'm the one with the sword. I can't protect you if you go running off."

Tabitha sniffed, licked her paw and started cleaning herself.

I lit a torch and looked around the room. There were stairs leading up and down. I decided to head upstairs first.

It was very boring. OK, so there were some nice views from some of the windows, but there was nothing exciting up here. I even tried to find a hidden room, knocking on the stones and seeing if there were any that were loose. Is this what I'd been so afraid of?

"Downstairs it is!"

I went down the stairs from the lobby. To my left I could see three levers. "I wonder what these do?"

I started pulling and pushing them at random. At one point, I thought I heard a distant click, but the levers didn't seem to do anything. After a while, I gave up.

There was a corridor leading away from the levers and I headed down it. So far, this temple was really disappointing. I almost wished there was a tentacle monster for some excitement.

Suddenly, Tabitha decided that she absolutely had to be petted and she rubbed herself across the front of my legs, making me trip over.

"Tabitha!"

"Meow."

I looked behind me and realized that Tabitha had saved me from a trap. Sticking out from the wall was an arrow that had been triggered when I'd walked over a tripwire.

"Thank you, Tabitha! That was close."

I followed the corridor round, paying close attention to where I put my feet. Good thing too – there was another tripwire just around the corner.

Tabitha put out one of her paws and, with a claw, cut the tripwire in half making the trap harmless. She really is a good friend.

There was a chest against the wall. Finally! There was bound to be some treasure inside.

I walked over to open the chest, but Tabitha hopped on top of it.

"Come on, Tabitha. Move out of the way. I want to see what's in the chest."

"Meow."

"Please, Tabitha? There could be treasure in there."

"Meow."

I sighed. "OK. Here's some fish." I pulled out some fish from my bag. It was getting late. No wonder she was feeling hungry.

Tabitha pounced on the fish, devouring it quickly. She didn't move from the chest, though.

"Here, Tabitha. Fetch the fish!" I tossed some more fish away from the chest, but Tabitha just blinked at me, as if to say 'I'm not a dog. Did you really think I'd fall for that?'

Instead, she curled up on top of the chest and purred herself to sleep.

There was nothing else to do but block up the corridor and join her. Still, it's not everyone who can say that they've spent the night in a jungle temple.

Day 15

I was woken up by Tabitha sitting on my chest, kneading it with her claws. "Get off!"

I'm sure that cat was laughing at me as I pushed her away.

Still, she wasn't sitting on the chest anymore, so I eagerly rushed over to open it. I couldn't believe my eyes. Gold! Emeralds! An enchanted book!

It had definitely been worth coming into the temple.

I unblocked the corridor and headed up the stairs to the lobby. Even though there hadn't been any monsters in the temple, there was something about it that made me uneasy and now that I'd seen everything there was to see. I wanted to get out of there.

"Meow!"

"Come on, Tabitha," I called over my shoulder. "It's time to go."

"Meow!"

I turned to see her standing by a hole in the ground by the stairs. I was sure that it hadn't been there when I arrived yesterday. Peering down, I thought that I could make out another chest.

"Stay here, Tabitha. I'll be right back."

I jumped down the hole. Sure enough, there was a second treasure chest. If it hadn't been for Tabitha, I would have missed it. She was going to get extra fish for dinner tonight!

Opening it up, I couldn't believe my luck. Diamonds! Lots and lots of diamonds!

I scooped them up and put them safely in my backpack. These were going to come in handy when it came to building my castle.

At last, the chest was empty and I climbed back out of the secret room to join Tabitha. "All right, Tabitha. Where are we going now? Do you know where there are any other temples?"

Tabitha shook her head.

"Maybe it's time to leave the jungle," I suggested. "It's been fun, but I haven't seen any other Minecraftians and it's pointless building a new shelter here if I still don't get any visitors. How do you feel about leaving?"

"Meow."

I picked up Tabitha, stroking her silky smooth fur. "I was hoping that you'd say that. Do you want to go back through the swamp or shall we try a different way?"

"Meow!"

Tabitha clearly hated the idea of the swamp. "OK, we'll see what else we can find on our way home. I have a great shelter. I think you're going to love it!"

I put Tabitha back down on the ground and she led the way out of the temple and into the sunlight.

Day 16

I must admit that I really loved having Tabitha with me as we meandered through the jungle. The cat is a real character!

When we sat down to eat lunch together, she'd reach out with her paw to pat my hand every time she wanted some more fish. Then when she'd finished eating, she'd knock her head against me, demanding that I stroke her. She could care less that I still had some food left to eat.

In the end, I had to stroke her with my left hand while I tried to eat my lunch with my right hand. Thank goodness it wasn't mushroom stew – that could have been really messy!

Sometimes she led the way down the path and sometimes I decided where we were going. We walked all day and we still didn't reach the end of the jungle, and by the time night fell, I was really tired. Too tired to build a shelter.

Tabitha meowed at me and sat down beside me, gazing out into the darkness. "Are you going to watch out for monsters?" I asked.

"Meow."

I took that as a yes and gratefully sank down on the ground, resting against a tree. I closed my eyes and was soon fast asleep.

Day 17

When I woke up, Tabitha was sitting exactly where she'd been the night before. "Have you been keeping watch all night?"

"Meow." Tabitha yawned and stretched, extending her sharp claws as far as they could go. If any monster had been foolish enough to try anything with her around, I didn't think they'd stand much of a chance against those sharp claws.

"You must be tired." I picked her up and she flopped against my chest, purring as I started walking with her cradled in my arms. There was something really rather sweet about having a pet cat to cuddle. I wish I'd met her sooner.

The only problem was that as Tabitha fell asleep, it made me sleepy too! I started yawning, struggling to put one foot in front of the other as my head kept nodding forward, despite a good night's rest.

When I saw a lake up ahead, I knew what I had to do. Our fish supplies were running a little low anyway, so I decided to rest up for the day and restock our food.

I propped my fishing line up on the ground next to me and laid back, Tabitha curled up on my chest.

That's how we spent the day. I'd snooze, waking up whenever I felt a fish nibbling at the line. Tabitha would move to one side so that I could reel it in. As soon as it was in my bag, she'd go straight back to lying on top of me, her purr soothing me off to sleep again.

This is the life!

Day 18

Thanks to our day of fishing, we had plenty of food and now it really was time to try and get back home. So far, I hadn't found anywhere I wanted to move my shelter to, but we were heading back along a different route to the one I'd taken to the jungle. There was still a chance that I'd find the perfect place to call home.

Having spent the whole day resting, we both had plenty of energy and Tabitha amused herself by disappearing off into the bushes, jumping out at me when I wasn't expecting it. She certainly kept me on my toes!

I smiled as I could hear her rustling in the bushes. "Tabitha, you silly cat. You're going to have be quieter if you're going to surprise me!"

GROAN!

A baby zombie came lurching through the undergrowth!

I pulled out my sword, but not before the zombie took a swipe at me, hitting me hard on the arm. Just because it was little didn't mean that it couldn't hurt me and I could barely move my arm, it was so sore.

I ran back a bit to give it a chance to recover before rushing at the zombie again, but before I could attack, a furious ball of fur came speeding out of the jungle and threw itself at the baby zombie!

I'd never seen anything like it. Tabitha was amazing! Yowling and screeching, she tore into the baby zombie and soon there was nothing left but a pile of rotting meat.

"Come on, Tabitha," I said to her. "We better get out of here. If there are any other zombies in the area, they'll be here soon and my arm is still aching too much to swing my sword."

Tabitha hissed at the remains of the baby zombie as she walked past, her tail held high.

Day 19

At last, the jungle trees started to give way to the more familiar oak and birch trees of a forest. Although we were still a long way from home, this was more like the kind of place I was used to and as I walked, I whistled a little tune, feeling happy to be somewhere that felt like home.

Up ahead, I could see a small shelter through the trees and I headed towards it, curious about who lived in this forest.

"Hello? Anyone home?" I knocked on the door, waiting for a reply.

Nothing.

I pushed at the door. It swung open. I poked my head through the doorway, looking around to see if the owner was in. "Hello? Is anyone there?"

"Who are you?"

I jumped and spun round. Standing in front of me was a Minecraftian, and he didn't look happy to see me. "My name's Steve. Pleased to meet you." I held out my hand for him to shake but he ignored me.

"Yes, well, Steve, you're on private property and I'd appreciate it if you left."

"Don't be like that. I just wanted to be friends."

"I don't need any friends. Now get off my land."

"Meow!" Tabitha weaved around my legs, rubbing her head against me affectionately.

"What's that?" asked the Minecraftian.

"That's my pet cat, Tabitha."

"Your pet cat? I've never seen anything like it." The Minecraftian seemed to lose his bad mood. "He's really cool."

"She," I corrected. "And her name's Tabitha."

"Tabitha, eh?" He nodded his head slowly. Thoughtfully. "Well, my name's Mike. I'm sorry for being so rude when you first arrived. I've had a lot of trouble with griefers recently."

"I understand. You can't be too careful these days."

"Well, Steve, you seem like a decent sort of fellow. Why don't you come in and stay for a while? I can put in a spare room for you. It would be good to have some company."

"That would be lovely," I smiled and helped Mike build a brand new room so I had somewhere to sleep while I stayed with him.

Day 20

Mike's really cool. He's been living out in the forest for a while, so his shelter is almost as good as mine, although he doesn't have a bath as big as a pool.

He does have a basketball hoop on the side of his house though and we spent all morning playing together. Mike beat me with one hand tied behind his back!

I'm going to put a basketball hoop on my shelter for practice. When he comes to visit, he won't find it nearly as easy to beat me.

Day 21

I'm really enjoying staying with Mike. Last night he cooked an amazing feast. I ate so much I felt like I could burst! He even had a whole pile of fish for Tabitha as well. She was very, very happy and purred loudly as she devoured them as if she hadn't eaten for months.

This morning, he took me round his farm to show me all the things he's growing. Even though we're not in the jungle anymore, he has a melon patch, as well as fields full of wheat, carrots, and potatoes. He told me it took ages to get the ground ready for planting, but it was worth it.

I must admit that although his melons don't taste quite as juicy as the ones in the jungle, they were still delicious. I've asked him to tell me all his secrets to growing melons so that I can have my own patch at home.

He's also got a whole heap of farm animals – pigs, cows, sheep, and chickens. Well, he did have a lot of chickens. That was before Tabitha caught sight of them. I've never seen her behave like this. She crouched down in the grass to stalk them, the only movement a very slight twitch in the tip of her tail. Then all of a sudden, she POUNCED!

The poor chickens didn't stand a chance. Luckily, Mike thought it was really funny otherwise we'd have had to leave. I would hate to lose one of the few friends I have. I know I should be heading back to my shelter to make sure that the diamonds are all still safe, but I'm having too much fun with Mike. I don't want to leave.

He says that he's going to show me his mine tomorrow and anything that I find down there I can keep. I can't wait!

Day 22

Mike is a sneaky, cheating, lowlife meanie. I hate him so much.

He took me to his mine this morning, just as he said he would. I left Tabitha back at his house. Mike had got a few more chickens for her to chase and he said it would be fine if she stayed behind and ate them.

It sounded like a good idea. After all, mines are dangerous places and I didn't want Tabitha to get hurt.

Mines are dangerous places all right, but if only I'd known what Mike was planning. Tabitha would have been perfectly safe if she'd been with me, instead of kidnapped – or should I say catnapped.

Mike led me into his mine, telling me all about a seam of diamonds he'd discovered just the other day. I'd told him all about my plans for a diamond museum and he promised that he'd come and visit when it was finished. He asked if I could put up a sign saying that he'd donated some of the diamonds and of course I agreed. It was the least I could do if he was going to let me have a whole heap of diamonds.

He led me down into the mine, deeper and deeper, all the way down to level 12 and beyond. At last, he stopped outside a dark cavern.

"If you go in there, you'll see the diamond ore straight ahead," he told me.

"Aren't you coming in with me?" I couldn't believe my luck. Mike was just going to let me have all the diamonds I could mine!

"No, no. You go first. I've already got as much as I wanted. Help yourself. I'll join you later – first I want to go and see if I can find some iron. I've got a few things I need to build and I don't have enough in my supplies."

"OK." I left Mike standing in the doorway as I stepped into the cavern. I could hardly breathe, I was so excited about all the diamonds I was going to find.

Mike had told me that the diamond ore was straight ahead, so I walked across the room. When I reached the other side, I couldn't see anything. I looked to my left. Nothing. I went over to my right. Nothing.

"Mike, where are the-"

BOOM!

The floor shook, the walls trembled, and the ceiling started to cave in at the sound of a massive explosion.

"Mike! Help me!" I was trapped, stuck under rubble and rocks.

Mike was nowhere to be seen, but I could have sworn that I could hear him laughing, the sound fading off into the distance as he walked away. I must have been mistaken. Mike wouldn't just leave me like this.

It seemed like forever before I was able to free my arms and start working away at the rocks pinning me down. At last I was able to get up from under the boulders, but I'd lost a lot of health and I was feeling really weak.

"Mike! Where are you? I need help!"

Perhaps Mike had been caught up in the explosion? Perhaps Mike was…

I didn't want to think about the worst happening to my friend.

"Mike! Mike! Where are you, Mike?" Even though I was feeling woozy, I started digging around, trying to find any sign of him. There was nothing. Just rocks and-

Wait a minute! Was that the remains of TNT?

I looked closer and sure enough, I could see a few scraps that looked suspiciously like explosives. Had Mike sent me into a trap?

I had a sinking feeling in the pit of my stomach. Tabitha! I'd left her back at Mike's house. Anything could have happened to her.

I got up to rush back to Mike's house, but I was still feeling weak and the best I could do was to shamble along. A zombie could have walked faster. If I had my backpack, I could have taken a potion of healing, but Mike had convinced me to leave it behind.

As I made my way up along the corridor we'd come down, the ground crumbled beneath me. I was on the verge of falling into a deep pit full of lava!

I edged around the pit, almost falling in a couple of times. I was sure that I was going the same way that we'd come, but there wasn't anything like this when Mike brought me into the mine.

When I came across a tripwire not much further along the corridor, there was no escaping the fact that Mike had deliberately set things up to hurt me.

But why?

Day 23

It seemed like forever before I was finally free of the mine, but at last I stumbled out into the daylight, blinking my eyes against the sudden bright light. I was lucky to still be alive. Mike had left every kind of trap imaginable along the way out, and it was only because I'd had to set so many traps myself because of the monsters around my home that I'd been able to avoid them all.

I don't think Mike expected me to survive the mine and now that I was free of its tunnels, I was going to get some answers.

My first instinct was to march over to his house and confront him, but I had a feeling that he'd be prepared for me. I was going to have to be cunning if I was going to find out why he was trying to kill me.

Tabitha! My poor, sweet kitty was somewhere out there with Mike. If he had tried to kill me, what was he trying to do to her? Was he eating cat soup by now?

I had to rescue her.

Day 24

Mike isn't as clever as he thinks he is. He seems to think that I didn't survive the mines. I've been watching him ever since I got out and he spent all day yesterday sitting on his porch with a sword by his side and a bow across his lap.

There was no sign of Tabitha.

This morning, he's back to his usual routine, so he's out in the fields tending to his crops. This gave me the chance to have a look around his house.

He's good at traps, I'll give him that, but I'm better. I could spot them all a mile away and it was easy to get around them to see if I could find Tabitha.

I can't believe that I ever thought that his house was cool. Mine's so much better. His is really small and it didn't take me long to go through every room looking for Tabitha, but there was no sign of her.

I'm starting to get really worried.

When Mike came home for lunch, I hid in a cupboard in his bedroom, listening to him moving about the place.

"How are you doing, my pretty new pet?" I heard him say. He must be talking to Tabitha!

I wanted to rush out and confront him, but I decided to stay where I was. There would be time for revenge later. I needed to be sure that Tabitha was safe first.

"Don't worry. You'll soon forget all about Steve, and then you'll be more than happy to eat the fish I bring you. I've even got a few chickens waiting for you. Not interested? Well, I'm sure you'll change your mind once you haven't eaten for a few days. In the meantime, I need you to go back into your hiding place, just in case. I'm pretty certain that Steve is lost in the mines and you'll never see him again, but if by some miracle he's still alive, I'll need to take care of him before I can let you run around the place."

There was a pause and I imagined Tabitha glaring at Mike. She was very good at letting you know when she wasn't happy.

"Not very talkative, are you? Steve told me that you meowed all the time. I guess he was making that up, just like he was making up his plans for a diamond museum. As if anyone would seriously want to build a diamond museum! What a stupid idea."

I couldn't believe what I was hearing. Mike had told me that it was a brilliant idea!

"Back in your box you go," said Mike. "I'll be back this evening and I'm warning you, cat. If you don't start being a little friendlier, I might just decide that you make a better dinner than you do a pet."

I gasped, then clapped a hand over my mouth, hoping that Mike didn't hear me. Luckily, he didn't seem to and as soon as I was sure that he was gone, I raced out of my hiding place, desperate to find Tabitha and get her out of here.

There was no sign of her.

"Looking for this?"

I whirled round. Mike was standing in the doorway holding up a cage with Tabitha sitting inside.

"Don't you hurt her!"

"Or you'll what?" Mike laughed. "You won't do anything to me and we both know it. So you survived the mines. You're still weak. I can tell by the way you move. You won't stand a chance against me. But I'm feeling generous today, so I'll let you walk out of here. After all, you did manage to avoid my traps. That does deserve a little bit of a reward."

"I'll walk out of here with Tabitha."

"Uh-uh-uh!" Mike tutted, wagging a finger at me. "This cat's mine now. My offer is for you and you alone."

"Meow!"

"I know, Tabitha. I'm trying my best, but what can I do? He's right. I am still weak. I don't even have a weapon. It's in my backpack, and I left it here when we went to the mines. All I can do is accept his offer and leave. I'm sorry."

"Meow!"

Tabitha's meow broke my heart as I walked out of the house and off into the forest.

Day 25

Of course I didn't really leave. I could never abandon my darling Tabitha like that! But I needed some time to recover and plan.

Mike might think that he'd won, but he'd reckoned without my years of experience in fighting off monsters around my shelter. If he thought that he knew a thing or two about setting traps, he hadn't seen anything yet. I was going to get my cat back and I didn't care what happened to Mike.

I spent the day watching and planning. I hadn't seen any sign of my backpack, so I was going to have to make do with wooden weapons made from the forest trees. I was so angry I felt as though I could destroy him with my bare hands, but I knew that I was going to have to act carefully if I was going to rescue Tabitha.

He'd left her cage out on the porch and I knew that she'd seen me hiding in the bushes from the way that her tail was twitching. She was a clever cat, though, and she knew that she couldn't do anything that would let Mike know where I was.

I ducked down into the bushes as Mike came out onto the porch with my backpack. "Let's see what Steve had in here, shall we?"

He tipped the contents out on the floor. It was all I could do not to rush out and tell him to be careful with my things, but I suspected that he was deliberately trying to annoy me in case I was watching. I stayed as still as a statue, biting my lip to stay quiet as he rummaged through my things.

"He's collected quite a bit of treasure, hasn't he? That'll be very useful. First a valuable new pet and now lots of gold and diamonds. I'm going to get a lot of money for you, cat. When people hear that I have a tamed ocelot, they're going to be desperate to get you for themselves and they'll pay me anything I ask. It was my lucky day when Steve came to visit."

His lucky day? We'll soon see about that.

Day 26

It had taken me a while to come up with it, but I finally had a plan and now I was crouched outside Mike's house disguised as a zombie. I'd covered my face with mud and dirt and I was really rather proud of the effect.

Hopefully it would fool Mike for long enough for me to be able to rescue Tabitha.

Now all I had to do was wait for the right moment.

Day 27

I jolted awake. I couldn't believe that I'd fallen asleep! I rushed around to Mike's bedroom window and breathed a sigh of relief when I saw that he was still in bed. Perfect.

I went round to the back of his house and set fire to the pile of wood that I'd put there last night before I fell asleep. Just as I thought it would, the flames quickly spread to the house.

"What? What? Fire! Fire!" I heard Mike leap out of bed and he rushed to the back door, opening it only to close it straight away when he saw how big the fire was.

Giggling, I tiptoed round to the front of the house, standing in front of the door.

"GROAN!" I yelled at Mike when he opened the door.

"Zombies!" He screamed and dropped everything he'd been carrying as he ran off into the forest.

"Stupid Mike. Doesn't he know that zombies burst into flames in sunlight?" I said to Tabitha as I carefully picked her up. Mike had dropped the cage she was in when he'd seen me. After everything he'd said about selling her, I knew he wouldn't leave her in a burning house.

"Come on, Tabitha, we need to get as far away from here as possible. I think it's time I took you back to my home, don't you?"

"Meow."

We walked away from Mike's burning house. By the time he realized he'd been fooled, there'd be nothing left of it but ashes and we'd be long gone. It served him right. After everything he'd done to me and Tabitha, he was lucky that I hadn't done worse.

Day 28

After all the excitement of the past few days, all I wanted to do was get home as quickly as possible. I'd given up any idea of scouting out somewhere new to live. Wherever I went, there was bound to be problems and I'd spent so long in building my shelter I hated the idea of starting all over again.

So what if I never had any visitors and nobody would want to come to a diamond museum surrounded by monsters? I had Tabitha for company and she was the best friend any Minecraftian could want.

It was going to take a long time for us to get back home and I wasn't looking forward to the walk, but at least I had Tabitha with me.

She'd been doing her usual thing of running around, disappearing off and then coming back when suddenly she came racing towards me. "Meow! Meow! Meow! Meow!"

Clearly she was very excited about something. "What is it, Tabitha?"

"Meow!"

"You want me to follow you?"

Tabitha turned and ran off and I raced after her, struggling to keep up. However, when I saw what she was so excited about, I could see why she'd been so keen to get me to come.

Horses! This would make getting home so much easier.

I'd tamed horses before, so I knew that I had to act cautiously. Still, I'd tamed an ocelot. A horse would be simple after that!

I went up to the nearest horse, holding my hands out so that they could see that they were empty.

The horse trotted over to me and when it was close enough, I leaped onto its back.

The horse whinnied and bucked me off.

Ouch! I landed right on my backside. It was very sore.

Still, I was determined to ride a horse all the way home, so I jumped onto its back again.

Once more, it bucked me off.

I lost count of how many times I climbed up onto its back only to have it kick me off again.

"Meow."

Tabitha came up to me, an apple in her mouth. She dropped it on the floor in front of me. Remembering how food had helped me tame her, I picked up the apple and gave it over to the horse, who snatched it greedily from my hand.

This time, when I got onto its back, it stood still. I motioned for Tabitha to jump up next to me, but she shook her head. Hoping that she'd be able to keep up, I kicked the horse and it started to trot, then canter, then gallop.

The wind blew through my hair, an incredible feeling as we raced towards my home.

"Meow!" I looked down and couldn't believe it. Tabitha was running just as fast as the horse, easily keeping pace with it. At this speed we'd soon be home.

By nightfall, we'd reached familiar land. I recognized the Extreme Hills that were near my shelter. I desperately wanted to get back home, but I knew the dangers of roaming around at night with all the monsters, so I put up a simple shelter to keep Tabitha and me safe. I set the horse free to go back to its friends – it wasn't fair to take it to my home where it would probably get eaten by zombies.

"This time tomorrow I'll be able to show you my home, Tabitha." The cat purred as I scratched her behind the ears before settling down to sleep.

Day 29

The night was surprisingly quiet. I was used to the sounds of creepers exploding, but I slept through undisturbed by strange explosions. Maybe I'd just slept more deeply than usual.

After a breakfast of the last of the fish I'd caught in the jungle, I picked up Tabitha and carried her down the hills and over to where my shelter was.

"There it is, Tabitha. Home, sweet home!" Tabitha meowed and raced over to get a closer look.

"Wait! Tabitha! There are traps!" I closed my eyes, not wanting to watch her trip one of the many traps I'd set up to keep away monsters and thieving Minecraftians, but I opened them again when I realized that I hadn't heard her set any of them off.

Sure enough, she'd reached my front door without triggering any of the traps.

"Clever girl," I smiled, stroking her back as she purred loudly. "Let's hope that nobody else was as talented as you. If someone's stolen my diamonds, I'll be very cross."

I went through my shelter, moving from room to room as I checked to see that everything was where I left it. It seemed that nobody was as skilful as Tabitha and all my treasure was exactly where it should be.

"Come on, Tabitha. Let's go fishing for supper. We'll have to keep our eyes open for creepers, though. They're everywhere around here."

Grabbing my fishing rod, I led Tabitha out through the back of the house and to the nearest lake. I wanted to show Tabitha my trick of using creepers to try and catch fish, but I couldn't see any around.

Not a single creeper. What was going on?

For the first time ever, I spent a relaxing afternoon fishing and by dinner time I had more than enough to treat Tabitha and cook for myself. I couldn't remember the last time I'd had an afternoon outside when I hadn't had to fight a monster of some kind or another.

"They must all be scared of you, Tabitha," I joked. "How silly of them. Don't they know you're just a soft little pussy cat?"

Tabitha said nothing. She just purred and purred.

Day 30

There's still no sign of any monsters. Maybe they've all moved away. It's very odd. Not that I'm complaining.

You see, I've had a brilliant idea. I've decided that I'm not going to build a diamond museum. Instead, I'm going to build a village! I don't know why I didn't think of it sooner. All this time I've been complaining that nobody comes to visit me, but I didn't do anything to make it easy for people to stay here.

So I'm going to build a brand new village with everything a Minecraftian needs to be happy. A weapon smith's, library, armory, you name it, I'm going to build it. I'm also going to flatten out the land by the lake for farming. The one good thing I got from Mike was how to grow melons and I'm determined to have fresh melon to eat.

If I can persuade some villagers to move in, they'll bring iron golems with them and iron golems are brilliant at fighting monsters. So even if the monsters do decide to come back, they won't stick around for long.

My shelter is going to be right at the center of the village, so I'll be able to see my friends all the time. I'm never going to be lonely again! And as a little thank you for being my friend, I'm going to leave a diamond inside every house. After all, if I'm not going to build my diamond museum, I don't need all those diamonds and what better way to welcome someone to a new home than to give them diamonds?

I wonder what happened to Mike. Maybe he got eaten by a real zombie. It would serve him right.

Meanwhile, I've got Tabitha by my side to help me build my village. She's already helped me start to get all the resources I need. She's my best friend in the whole wide world. I bet we're going to have lots more adventures together. I only wish I could show her how much fun you can have with a creeper, but they appear to be afraid of my ferocious Tabitha!

27759502R00046

Printed in Great Britain
by Amazon